*Cornerstones of Freedom*

# The Titanic

Deborah Kent

CHILDREN'S PRESS
A Division of Grolier Publishing
Sherman Turnpike
Danbury, Connecticut 06816

Library of Congress Cataloging-in-Publication Data

Kent, Deborah.
 The Titanic / by Deborah Kent.
  p. cm. — (Cornerstones of freedom)
 Summary: Describes the disastrous 1912 sinking of the
world's largest ocean liner after colliding with an
iceberg during its maiden voyage.
  ISBN 0-516-46672-0
 1. Titanic (Steamship)—Juvenile literature.
2. Shipwrecks—North Atlantic Ocean—Juvenile
literature. [1. Titanic (Steamship) 2. Shipwrecks.]
I. Title. II. Series.
G530.T6K46 1993
910'.91634—dc20                                         93-12688
[B]                                                          CIP
                                                              AC

17 18 19 20 R 17 16 15

The sea was glassy calm as the great British steamship *Titanic* plowed through the North Atlantic on its journey from Southampton, England, to New York. On April 14, 1912, the *Titanic* was four days into its maiden voyage. By now, passengers and crew had settled contentedly into the shipboard routine. After dinner in first class, several women passengers sang hymns in the reception room. Men gathered in the smoking room to play cards. Jack Thayer, a seventeen-year-old from Pennsylvania, walked the promenade deck with a friend, Milton Long. They had just met at dinner, but already they felt like old friends—discussing the state of the world, their lives, their plans for the future.

*Passengers strolling on the deck of the* Titanic

The Titanic's
luxurious
first-class
staterooms
were nearly
identical to
those on the
Olympic
(right), the
Titanic's
sister ship.

"OLYMPIC." FIRST CLASS SUITE STATEROOM.

So far the trip seemed smooth and uneventful.
Yet a spirit of excitement hovered around the
ship. This was a special voyage, a triumph of
man's ingenuity over the forces of nature.

Never before in the history of seafaring had so
large and splendid a vessel been launched. The
*Titanic* measured 882 feet from bow to stern—
nearly as long as three football fields. From its
keel to the top of its four enormous funnels, it
was as tall as an eleven-story building. And, for
its first-class passengers, it was equipped with
every possible luxury. French chefs prepared
sumptuous meals, served on fine china in the
elegant, carpeted dining room. There were
beauty salons, a Turkish bath, a gymnasium, a

The Titanic was equipped with every possible luxury, including (clockwise from top left) an elegant first-class dining saloon offering a gourmet menu; a Turkish bath; a gymnasium; and a spectacular Grand Staircase.

*John Jacob Astor*

squash court, a darkroom, and even a freshwater swimming pool—one of the first aboard an ocean liner. The great ship had attracted some of the richest members of British and American society. Its passenger list included Benjamin Guggenheim, whose family had made its fortune in smelting; Isidor Straus, owner of New York's Macy's department store; and New York real-estate tycoon John Jacob Astor.

The *Titanic*'s second-class quarters were not as lavish as those for first-class passengers, but they

*The* Titanic's *second-class cabins were very comfortable by 1912 standards.*

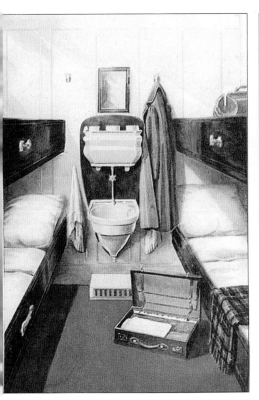

*Even the* Titanic's *third-class cabins (left) and dining room (right) surpassed those of other passenger ships of the time.*

still permitted travelers to sail in comfort. Even the third-class, or steerage, accommodations, far below decks near the bottom of the ship, were spacious compared to those on other British vessels. Each steerage cabin had four bunks and a washbasin. But the ceilings in steerage were crisscrossed with pipes and girders. In first class, the inner workings of the ship were discreetly covered with wood paneling. Only the steady hum of the engines reminded the wealthy that they were at sea.

The White Star Line, which owned and operated the *Titanic,* was especially proud of the

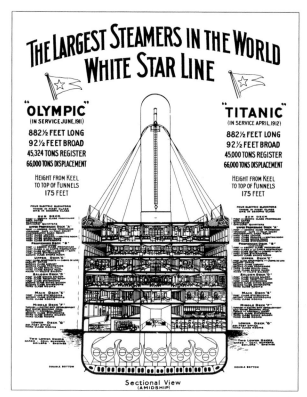

*Right: Captain Smith (at right) on deck with Lord James Pirrie,
the shipbuilder whose idea it was to build the* Olympic *and* Titanic
*Left: An advertisement describing the dimensions of the two ships*

ship's safety features. A double bottom provided extra protection if the hull were damaged. In an emergency, sixteen watertight compartments could be closed off with the flick of a switch. Furthermore, the *Titanic* exceeded the British Trade Commission's lifeboat requirements, providing enough space for 1,200 people. Although the *Titanic* actually carried some 2,200 passengers and crew members, no one worried. Most people believed the *Titanic* was unsinkable.

Even the *Titanic*'s captain, Edward J. Smith, may have thought he commanded an unsinkable ship. He did not seem especially concerned when, at 11:20 A.M., the *Titanic's* radio operators picked up a message from a German ship warning of drifting icebergs. As the day passed, Smith received several more radio messages about ice along his route. Yet the *Titanic* rushed forward, full speed ahead at 21 knots. At that time, it was common practice for ships to travel at full speed through areas where ice had been spotted, trusting the ability of the ship's lookouts to spot icebergs in time to avoid a collision.

Every year, about a thousand icebergs drift through the shipping lanes off Newfoundland's Grand Banks. They are vast islands of ice, some towering two hundred feet into the air. Icebergs

*Newfoundland's "iceberg alley"*

*Watchman Frederick Fleet*

are especially treacherous for ships because most of their bulk lies hidden beneath the ocean's surface. They are pitilessly solid, immovable, and indestructible.

Late in the evening, the *Titanic* came within radio range of the relay station at Cape Race, Newfoundland. This meant that for the first time, the ship had direct communication with the North American continent. Radio operator Jack Phillips was deluged with passenger messages—birthday wishes, stock-market news, family gossip. At about 11:00 P.M., the British ship *Californian*, about ten miles away, broke in with another warning about icebergs. "Shut up, shut up," the overworked Phillips tapped back impatiently in Morse code. "I am busy. I am working Cape Race." The ice message went undelivered to the ship's bridge.

In the crow's nest, watchman Frederick Fleet scanned the horizon. The night was clear and bright with stars, but Fleet wished he had a pair of binoculars. He had been asking for them ever since the ship left Southampton, but somehow they had been mislaid.

Suddenly, at 11:40 P.M., Fleet sighted an ominous black mass looming in the *Titanic*'s path. He snatched up the telephone that connected the crow's nest with the bridge and shouted to First Officer William Murdoch, "Iceberg right ahead!"

*The moment of impact, as depicted by artist Melbourne Brindle*

Instantly Murdoch went into action. "Hard a' starboard!" he ordered, turning the ship sharply to port. He pulled the switch to close the watertight compartments below decks and ordered the ship to put its engines in reverse. But in the next moment, he felt a sickening jolt. The warning had come an instant too late.

Back in his cabin, Jack Thayer felt the impact, but it was so slight he could not believe anything was seriously wrong. "If I had had a brimful glass of water in my hand, not a drop would have been spilled," he recalled later. He told his parents he was going up on deck "to see the fun."

As soon as Murdoch reported what had happened, Captain Smith went below to survey the damage. He was accompanied by Thomas Andrews, who had helped design the *Titanic* for the shipbuilding firm Harland and Wolff. Andrews was a perfectionist. In a recent letter to his wife, he had lamented the *Titanic*'s flaws— space was wasted in the reading room on the promenade deck, the wicker deck furniture should have been stained green, and there were too many screws in the stateroom hat racks.

Harland and Wolff had built the *Titanic* to stay afloat if any two of its watertight compartments should be flooded. It could survive even if the first four were damaged. Now, to their horror, Smith and Andrews saw that the ship's design had not gone far enough. The iceberg had caused a two-hundred-foot rupture along the great ship's

*Contrary to popular belief, the iceberg did not–as this artist thought–rip a gash in the ship; rather, it pressed against the hull's seams, causing its rivets to pop and allowing water to gush in through a two hundred-foot rupture.*

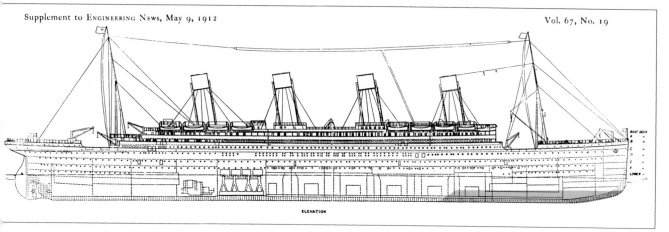

Supplement to Engineering News, May 9, 1912

Vol. 67, No. 19

ELEVATION

*Water immediately flooded the first six watertight compartments.*

starboard flank, and the sea invaded six of the watertight compartments. The bulkheads (walls) separating the compartments went only as high as the fifth-deck level. As the rushing water tilted the bow forward, the rear compartments would inevitably fill one by one like the sections of an ice-cube tray.

Within twenty minutes of the collision, Andrews and Smith knew the worst. They faced an inconceivable catastrophe. The biggest ship in the world, the unsinkable *Titanic,* was doomed.

At first, few of the passengers or crew members suspected that their lives were in danger. Lawrence Beesley, a schoolteacher traveling in second class, noticed that the steady hum of the engines had ceased, and heard the loud hiss of escaping steam. He asked a steward why the ship had stopped. "I don't know sir," the steward replied, "but I don't suppose it's much."

Some of the passengers found piles of ice heaped in the forward well deck—the exercise deck used by the people in third class. In high spirits, a crowd of young men kicked chunks of ice around the deck in a boisterous game of soccer.

Meanwhile, Captain Smith gathered the ship's officers. They listened in disbelief as he explained that the *Titanic* was going down. At best, she would stay afloat for another two hours. In filling the lifeboats, the captain commanded the officers to follow the time-honored custom of the sea— women and children first.

From the beginning, Smith and the officers knew that there could be fearsome casualties. Even if every lifeboat were filled to capacity, a thousand people would be left on the sinking ship. Their only hope lay in keeping the *Titanic* afloat as long as possible, until another ship came to the rescue.

In the radio room, Jack Phillips was about to turn in for the evening. Suddenly the captain appeared in the doorway and informed him that the *Titanic* was in dire trouble. He must try to contact any ship within range and signal for aid.

Phillips set to work at once. For a time, he tapped out the letters "CQD," which ships had used for years to call for assistance. But after a while, he decided to try a new signal that had just been approved for use by international radio operators. Urgently, he tapped out: "Dot dot dot, dash dash dash, dot dot dot." It was one of

*From a radio room like this (left), Jack Phillips (above, in hat) telegraphed for help. Phillips died that night, though his assistant, Harold Bride (top), survived.*

the first times that the now-standard call "SOS" was used to summon help for a ship in distress.

Fearing the passengers would panic, the crew sounded no general alarm. Some people learned of the trouble from stewards who knocked on their stateroom doors, advising them to put on lifejackets. Others went on deck to investigate the commotion, and picked up rumors wherever they could. Far below in steerage, many of the passengers did not speak English. In Armenian, Italian, Finnish and Czech they questioned each other, but no one had many answers.

*"Women and children first" was the rule as anxious passengers entered the lifeboats.*

*Second Officer Herbert Lightoller*

Up on deck, Second Officer Herbert Lightoller and the crew began loading women and children into the lifeboats. Entering the boats was a frightening and perilous procedure. As the sinking ship leaned more and more to starboard, the lifeboats on that side swung far out over the water on their davits. Some terrified mothers and sobbing children crawled to the swaying boats across precarious bridges made of deck chairs. The boats then had to be lowered as much as seventy-five feet from the slanting deck to the sea.

Many people did not want to enter the lifeboats, finding it hard to grasp that the *Titanic* was in real trouble. Some passengers saw lights ahead, and assured each other that help was near. Many experts believe that the lights came from the *Californian*, which may still have been only ten miles from the *Titanic*. But by the time Phillips began calling for help, the *Californian*'s radio had shut down for the night. The closest vessel to respond was the *Carpathia*, fifty-eight miles away. Immediately, the *Carpathia*'s captain altered his course and steamed toward the *Titanic* at top speed.

*These two young boys survived the sinking; their father did not.*

At 1:15 A.M., Captain Stanley Lord of the *Californian* was awakened by his ship's second officer. The officer told Lord that he and several crewmen had seen a series of white rockets flash across the night sky. They might be distress

*The* Carpathia *was the closest ship to respond to the* Titanic's *call.*

signals from a ship whose lights had been sighted a few miles off. The *Californian*'s crew had attempted to signal to the ship with a Morse lamp, but received no response. No one thought to wake up the *Californian*'s radio operator. After questioning the officer at some length, Lord concluded that the rockets were probably just standard company signals. In 1912, each shipping firm had a unique signal rocket for announcing itself to nearby vessels.

Captain Lord dismissed the officer, crawled back into his bunk, and fell asleep. A few miles away, the *Titanic* launched yet another white rocket toward the heavens, and awaited a reply that did not come.

While crew members maneuvered women and children into the lifeboats, word of the danger filtered down to the third-class passengers. Many accepted their fate with resignation. A Swedish immigrant, August Wennerstrom, later recalled, "Hundreds were in a circle with a preacher in the middle, praying, crying, asking God and Mary to help them. They lay there still crying till the water was over their heads."

Other third-class passengers fought for their lives. The swaying iron stairways rang beneath their stampeding feet as they wound their tortuous way up and up. Several times, locked gates barred their path. But they burst through the barriers, while crewmen shouted that they

Most passengers who died in the disaster were in third class; their exit was made difficult by locked passageways, a maze of staircases, and general confusion. Many passengers also refused to leave their cabins, not believing the ship was in danger.

would be prosecuted for damaging White Star property. White Star officials later claimed that the company provided equal protection for all passengers, rich and poor alike. But somehow, the precious seats in the boats went mainly to people who had paid first- or second-class fares.

In violation of the strict code of the sea, a number of adult male passengers (most of them from first and second class) were given seats in the boats, while many women and children (mainly from third class) were left behind. One

*H. Bruce Ismay, director of the White Star Line*

such first-class survivor was White Star managing director H. Bruce Ismay. In the confusion, Ismay found himself on a nearly deserted section of the deck just as a boat was about to be lowered. No women or children were in sight, and he scrambled aboard.

The *Titanic* had sixteen full-size lifeboats and four smaller collapsible craft. There had never been a lifeboat drill on the unsinkable ship, and most of the crewmen were bewildered by the complicated launching process. As the water rose below decks, fear mounted that the boats would not be lowered in time. Spurred by panic, the crew did not wait to fill each boat to its capacity. Lifeboats designed to hold sixty-five people set off with only thirty-five or forty. One boat, meant to carry forty, left the *Titanic* with only twelve people aboard.

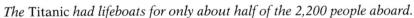

*The* Titanic *had lifeboats for only about half of the 2,200 people aboard.*

*Isidor and Ida Straus (left) and Benjamin Guggenheim (right)*

Many people did not attempt to save themselves, but faced death with courage and dignity. When Ida Straus, wife of millionaire Isidor Straus, was offered the chance to enter a boat, she refused to leave her husband. "We have been living together for many years," she told him. "Where you go, I go." Isidor, too, refused to get into a boat, though crewmen argued that he was elderly and no one would begrudge him a place. The Strauses settled side by side on deck chairs, quietly awaiting the end together.

Another millionaire, Benjamin Guggenheim, appeared on deck in elegant evening clothes, as though he were heading for the theater. He told one of the stewards to give his wife the message that he had died like a gentleman.

The longer the *Titanic* stayed afloat, the more lives might be spared. Engine-room workers fought to keep the pumps running at full speed. Knee deep in icy water, engineers labored over the generators to keep the ship's lights burning till the last possible moment. In the radio room, Jack Phillips worked on, even after the captain gave him permission to abandon his post. Perhaps he was stricken with remorse over his cavalier response to the *Californian*'s ice warning —a warning that might have saved them all.

As the deck tilted more and more steeply, the ship's band leader gathered his eight musicians. While the lifeboats disappeared one by one, the band played a series of jaunty ragtime tunes. The music floated bright and clear across the water, a last message of hope.

*In the boiler rooms, which looked like this (right), crewmen kept the power up, while the band (left) played on deck to calm the passengers.*

 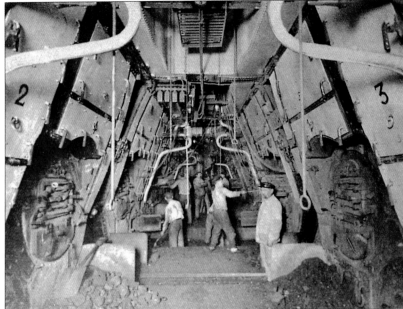

*The Titanic's stern rose dramatically as the bow sank lower and lower.*

At 2:05 A.M., the *Titanic* gave a dreadful lunge, and water rushed up the deck. Jack Thayer and Milton Long decided it was time to jump from the sinking ship. Long swung over the rail and let himself drop. Seconds later, Thayer followed his friend into the sea.

At 28 degrees Fahrenheit, the water was achingly cold. But somehow Thayer managed to reach an overturned lifeboat. Several other men clung there already, and someone helped him out of the water. He looked around for Long, but his friend had vanished forever.

*Thomas Andrews, the ship's designer (above), was last seen standing alone in the smoking room (right).*

On the *Titanic*, Captain Smith released the crew, saying they had done their full duty and could do no more. "It's every man for himself now," he told them. Softly, he added, "That's the way of it at this kind of time . . ." Smith made no effort to save himself. He waited on the bridge to go down with his ship.

Thomas Andrews, the ship's designer, stood alone in the smoking room. "Aren't you going to have a try for it, sir?" a passing steward asked him. Andrews did not reply. No one ever saw him again.

The last lifeboat splashed into the water, leaving more than 1,500 people stranded on the doomed ship. As waves swept over the deck, people scrambled astern and clung to their final refuge above the water. Most of them were men, but more than 150 women and children had not found places in the boats. A priest moved among them, administering last rites.

The end was very near when the band began its final offering. It shifted from sprightly ragtime pieces to a solemn hymn called "Autumn," a haunting farewell to the world of the living.

At 2:18 A.M., the *Titanic*'s bow plunged under the water. A horrible roar could be heard as all movable objects inside the ship—from tables, chairs, beds, luggage, and countless pieces of silver and china, to five grand pianos—crashed toward the sinking bow. The ship's lights blinked once, and went out forever. But the great ship could not bear the stress of having its stern tilted up in the air. As the people in lifeboats watched

*The* Titanic's *final plunge*

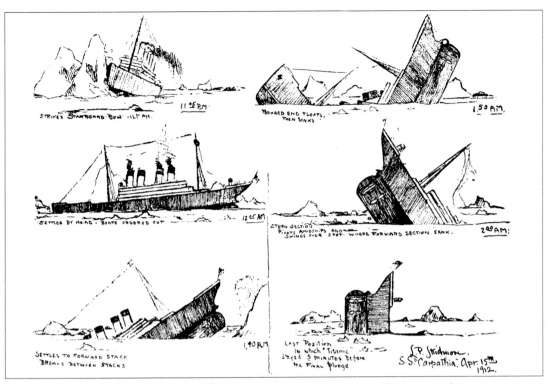

*Based on Jack Thayer's description, a passenger on the rescue ship* Carpathia *sketched this diagram of the* Titanic's *final hours.*

in horror, the *Titanic* broke in two between its third and fourth funnels. The front half of the ship disappeared into the water.

From a lifeboat, Officer Lightoller witnessed the *Titanic's* last moments. "The lights suddenly went out. . . . Slowly and almost majestically, the immense stern reared itself up . . .till at last she assumed the exact perpendicular. Then with an ever-quickening glide, she slid beneath the water of the cold Atlantic. . . . Every one of us had been spellbound by the sight, and as she disappeared, the words were breathed, 'She's gone.'"

It was 2:20 A.M., less than three hours after Frederick Fleet sighted the deadly iceberg.

As the great ship sank from view, hundreds of people spilled into the freezing water. Buoyed by lifejackets, they floundered helplessly in the numbing cold. As he clung to the hull of the overturned lifeboat, Jack Thayer heard their cries for help, "one continuous, wailing chant . . . like locusts on a midsummer night." A few of the partially filled lifeboats rowed back and rescued as many people as they could. But most of the survivors feared their boats would be swamped by the desperate swimmers. They sat listening to the desperate pleas, resolutely doing nothing, until at last the sounds faded into silence.

At about 4:00 A.M., the *Carpathia* reached the

*Those who were lucky enough to have a spot in one of the* Titanic's *lifeboats waited on the open sea for nearly two hours before help arrived.*

*A Titanic lifeboat is hoisted aboard the Carpathia.*

site of the tragedy and took the survivors aboard. Some of the people in the lifeboats had died of exposure.

The world reeled in disbelief at news of the *Titanic* disaster. Headlines blazed with the names of the rich and famous who had been lost. In all, more than fifteen hundred people had gone down with the ship. Hadn't modern engineering made such a calamity impossible?

The tragedy seemed so preventable. If only the captain had heeded the iceberg warnings! If only the watchman had had binoculars! If only the *Californian* had recognized the distress signals! Hungry for someone to blame, the public pointed at Captain Smith for sailing too fast in an icy

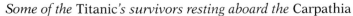

*Some of the* Titanic's *survivors resting aboard the* Carpathia

"All the News That's Fit to Print"

# The New York Times.

THE WEATHER.

VOL. LXI...NO. 19,806.   NEW YORK, TUESDAY, APRIL 16, 1912—TWENTY-FOUR PAGES.   ONE CENT

## TITANIC SINKS FOUR HOURS AFTER HITTING ICEBERG; 866 RESCUED BY CARPATHIA, PROBABLY 1250 PERISH; ISMAY SAFE, MRS. ASTOR MAYBE, NOTED NAMES MISSING

**Col. Astor and Bride, Isidor Straus and Wife, and Maj. Butt Aboard.**

**"RULE OF SEA" FOLLOWED**

Women and Children Put Over in Lifeboats and Are Supposed to be Safe on Carpathia.

**PICKED UP AFTER 8 HOURS**

Vincent Astor Calls at White Star Office for News of His Father and Leaves Weeping.

**FRANKLIN HOPEFUL ALL DAY**

Manager of the Line Insisted Titanic Was Unsinkable Even After She Had Gone Down.

**HEAD OF THE LINE ABOARD**

The Lost Titanic Being Towed Out of Belfast Harbor.

CAPT. E. J. SMITH, Commander of the Titanic.

**PARTIAL LIST OF THE SAVED.**

Includes Bruce Ismay, Mrs. Widener, Mrs. H. B. Harris, and an Incomplete names, suggesting Mrs. Astor's.

**Biggest Liner Plunges to the Bottom at 2:20 A. M.**

**RESCUERS THERE TOO LATE**

Except to Pick Up the Few Hundreds Who Took to the Lifeboats.

**WOMEN AND CHILDREN FIRST**

Cunarder Carpathia Rushing to New York with the Survivors.

**SEA SEARCH FOR OTHERS**

The Californian Stands By on Chance of Picking Up Other Boats or Rafts.

**OLYMPIC SENDS THE NEWS**

Only Ship to Flash wireless Messages to Shore After the Disaster.

*News of the tragedy reached a horrified world the next day.*

region, and at Bruce Ismay for saving himself when so many others died.

As a result of the disaster, new regulations were passed to make passenger liners safer. All ships were required to have enough lifeboats to hold everyone on board. Ships carrying more than fifty people were required to have lifeboat drills and a twenty-four-hour radio watch. Never again would an ice message be allowed to go undelivered to a ship's bridge. And, in 1913, the International Ice Patrol was formed to warn ships of icebergs in the North Atlantic sea lanes.

*Dr. Robert Ballard*

*One of hundreds of items found on the ocean floor near the wreck*

*Many people objected when, after Ballard's discovery, another expedition removed relics from the site.*

Over the decades, the story of the *Titanic* became a legend, capturing the imagination of the Western world. Many books and two major movies explored the story in poignant detail. Though a number of attempts were made to find the sunken ship, her exact location remained a mystery. Then, in 1985, oceanographers Robert Ballard and Jean-Louis Michel discovered the long-lost *Titanic*. At last, cameras on an unmanned underwater vessel sent back eerie, fuzzy pictures of the wreck, resting two-and-a-half miles down on the ocean floor. The next year, Dr. Ballard returned to explore the site in a special submarine equipped with a high-tech camera. With dazzling clarity, Ballard's photographs revealed remnants of the *Titanic*'s grand staircase, the crow's nest, the ship's boilers. Relics of shipboard life were strewn around the shattered hull—trays and wine bottles, bedsprings and lumps of coal, dishes, a doll's head, and even a chamber pot. Before leaving the site, Ballard held a brief memorial service for the dead and hoisted the flag of the shipbuilding firm Harland and Wolff.

For a time, there was talk of raising the great ship, perhaps restoring it as a museum. But engineering experts agreed that it would be an impossible feat. As one remarked, "Rather than raise the *Titanic*, it would be easier to lower the Atlantic." Besides, most people agreed that the

*An underwater camera provides a glimpse of the long-lost* Titanic.

underwater wreck should be thought of as a memorial that ought to be left undisturbed.

The *Titanic* lives on as a symbol of human pride and human failure, heroism and pathos. Looking back at the tragedy many years later, Jack Thayer wrote, "It seems to me that the disaster . . . not only made the world rub its eyes and awake, but woke it with a start, keeping it moving ever since with less and less peace, satisfaction and happiness. In my mind, the world of today awoke April 15, 1912."

## INDEX

## PHOTO CREDITS

Cover, © Chris Mayger, R.S.M.A.; 1, Courtesy of The Mariners' Museum, Newport News, VA; 2, 3, © Thomas Colletta; 4, 5 (top left), Ken Marschall; 5 (top right), Don Lynch; 5 (middle), Courtesy of the Mariners' Museum, Newport News, VA; 5 (bottom left), Ulster Folk & Transport Museum, © Reman Property, Harland & Wolff Ltd.; 5 (bottom right), Brown Brothers; 6 (top), UPI/Bettmann; 6 (bottom), 7 (right), © National Maritime Museum, London; 7 (left), collection of Titanic Historical Society; 8 (left), Courtesy of The Mariners Museum, Newport News, VA; 8 (right), North Wind; 9, © John Eastcott/Yva Momatiuck/Valan Photos; 10, Bettmann/Hulton; 11, H.M.S. *Titanic*, painted by Melbourne Brindle; 12, The Bettmann Archive; 13, Courtesy of The Mariners' Museum, Newport News, VA; 15 (left), The Bettmann Archive; 15 (top right, bottom right), *The Illustrated London News* Picture Library; 16 (top), The Bettmann Archive; 16 (bottom), Courtesy of The Mariners' Museum, Newport News, VA; 17 (top), AP/Wide World; 17 (bottom), UPI/Bettmann; 19, *The Illustrated London News* Picture Library; 20 (top), Bettmann/Hulton; 20 (bottom), *Cork Examiner;* 21 (left), Walter Lord Collection; 21 (right), The Bettmann Archive; 22 (left), *The Illustrated London News* Picture Library; 22 (right), Ken Marschall; 23, UPI/Bettmann; 24 (left), Ken Marschall; 24 (right), Courtesy of The Mariners' Museum, Newport News, VA; 25, The Bettmann Archive; 26, *The Illustrated London News* Picture Library; 27, Stock Montage; 28 (top), UPI/Bettmann; 28 (bottom), Bettmann/Hulton; 29, The Bettmann Archive; 30, AP/Wide World; 31, © Woods Hole Oceanographic Institution

Picture Identifications:
Cover: A painting of the *Titanic* during her final hours by Chris Mayger, R.S.M.A.
Page 1: Anguished wives enter the *Titanic's* lifeboats, knowing they would probably never see their husbands again
Page 2: A painting of the *Titanic* by Thomas Colletta

Project Editor: Shari Joffe
Designer: Karen Yops
Photo Research: Jan Izzo
Cornerstones of Freedom Logo: David Cunningham

## ABOUT THE AUTHOR

**Deborah Kent** grew up in Little Falls, New Jersey, and received her B.A. from Oberlin College. She earned a master's degree in social work from Smith College, and worked for four years at the University Settlement House on New York's Lower East Side.

Ms. Kent left social work to begin a career in writing. She published her first novel, *Belonging*, while living in San Miguel de Allende, Mexico. She has written a dozen novels for young adults. As well as numerous nonfiction titles for children. She lives in Chicago with her husband and their daughter Janna.